Casting Down Imaginations

Dr. Marlene Miles

Freshwater Press 2024

Freshwaterpress9@gmail.com

ISBN: 978-1-963164-48-0

Paperback Version

Table of Contents

CASTING DOWN IMAGINATIONS

Freshwater

For though we walk in the flesh, we do not war
after the flesh:

(For the weapons of our warfare are not carnal,
but mighty through God to the pulling down of
strong holds)

Casting down imaginations, and every high
thing that exalteth itself against the knowledge
of God, and bringing into captivity every
thought to the obedience of Christ;

And having in a readiness to revenge all
disobedience, when your obedience is fulfilled.

(2 Corinthians 2:3-6)

Casting Down Imaginations

Casting down imaginations, and every high
thing that exalteth itself against the knowledge
of God, and bringing into captivity every
thought to the obedience of Christ;
(2 Corinthians 10:5)

Right out the box I will give you the definition of witchcraft: It is evil imagination against another person and the willingness to carry it out **by any means.** Once the devil knows your level of desperation or determination, he's got you! He will offer all kinds of demonic solutions to what you've decided is a problem.

The thoughts of the wicked [are] an
abomination to the LORD: but [the words] of
the pure [are] pleasant words. (Proverbs 15:26)

Who do you think the wicked are? Yes, the heart of man is deceitfully wicked, and we all need to repent – but evil human agents, witches, warlocks, and wizards are constantly planning evil and are not content unless they are doing just that or destroying a soul ---and they **are surely wicked, and they are an abomination to the LORD.**

> For they sleep not, except they have done mischief; and their sleep is taken away, unless they cause some to fall. (Proverbs 4:16)

Consider the above verse in a multifaceted way. Some are so angry or so determined to do evil, they may be in a blind rage to commit their revenge or strike against another that their sleep is taken from them. On the other hand, those who are initiated into covens and darkness must do certain evil, that is, certain amounts of evil before they can sleep. Also, they do this evil in the dark, after midnight, and they can't rest until it is completed, or they will have hell to pay. Of course, they will have hell to pay, sooner or later, or both sooner and later. That is the cost for using the devil for anything --, anything at all.

What are they doing up all night like that? Casting spells, casting incantations, casting evil--, yes, casting evil imaginations. They are putting into the spirit what they imagine for the life of their victim and these imaginings are exalted against the knowledge of God for the life of their intended victim.

Let's read the verse before 2 Cor 10:3-6

For though we walk in the flesh, we do not war
after the flesh. (For the weapons of our warfare
are not carnal, but mighty through God to the
pulling down of strong holds) Casting down
imaginations, and every high thing that
exalteth itself against the knowledge of God,
and bringing into captivity every thought to the
obedience of Christ; And having in a readiness
to revenge all disobedience, when your
obedience is fulfilled.

Verse 4, For the weapons of our warfare are
not carnal, but mighty through God to the
pulling down of strongholds.

A stronghold is a position, a building or a
place that is strongly defended. That means
something like a fort, a military base, a walled
city, or even a willful or closed mind that believes
what it wants, and no one can change it. A
hardened heart of the variety that Pharoah had is
a stronghold. After 10 plagues were sent to
change that heart/mind and still Pharaoh and his
army pursued and we drorewned. Pharoah
believes what he believes and does what he likes
while saying, *Who is this God of yours?*

God is a high tower that the righteous can
run into and be safe; He is our stronghold. He is

our shelter; in Him is protection, safety, and peace.

In the New Testament Apostle Paul mentions strongholds of the mind intimating that these fortifications drive or control a man to certain actions or inactions in his life. They are described as being against God or higher than the knowledge of God. There is no knowledge higher than God, but demonic knowledge purports itself as that, dark counsel is deception and therefore disregards, dishonors and disrespects the Knowledge of God. God-knowledge IS the Spirit of Knowledge and the Spirit of Wisdom; there is none higher.

Whether you are present in real time or not when evil imaginations are being sent against you, you still have the right, the authority and the responsibility to cast them down. That is accomplished by prayers, declarations, and decrees.

You know how you can rent a room at a hotel or a library, or open up a chat room online? Witchcraft seeks to *open up a room in a person's mind (life)*; lodge there and either create or cause the person to create a stronghold in their own mind to let that incantation, hex, vex, spell or whatever was used to get locked in. You've heard folk say that So & So is living rent-free in your mind? Yeah, they, or you have opened up a room in your mind for this person. Thinking about them all the time is idolatry and creates soul ties. People under witchcraft attack—it's all they can think about because they are trying to use their mind to either understand or solve what has happened to them, either suddenly or insidiously and MAKE IT STOP. But the more time you spend on it, the more it is *worshipped* and gets embedded in there.

The proper counter is the Word of God, either read, prayed, decreed, declared, or ministered to you as by deliverance to unlock that stronghold.

Do you recall the lock bridge in Paris where lovers strolled and put their lock on the bridge for posterity? It is named the Pont des Arts Bridge, it was world-famous, but a part of it collapsed from the weight of the padlocks attached to it. Those locks weren't going anywhere on their own except by an outside force. Strongholds especially created by witchcraft attack are that way.

Rooms--, ways of thought, even hardened ways of thought that are padlocked and controlling and damaging to a soul, relationships, marriage, education, career, and life are so heavy they also can cause a collapse. This must be dealt with before that happens.

Spiritual Weapons

So, we need a *spiritual weapon* to get a negative thought out of our mind? Shall we take out a spiritual weapon to shoot it at ourselves? Of course, not. What, are we going to fire it at the thought? Or do we fire it at the padlock that is locking in an evil thought? If that is the case, do we *really* need a spiritual weapon to change our mind or our mindset?

If we need such spiritual fire power, then aren't we admitting that there is something in us that is causing the thought versus ourselves having the thought on our own? If you thought a thought, can't you just *unthink* it?

Depends. Perhaps one that has been in your bloodline for generations is a stronghold or your mind has developed strongholds, and that crazy thought is locked away in it. How do you get that thought *out*? It's more complicated than getting a song stuck in your head and you can't get it out. I race to the volume control of the TV or radio to make sure I don't hear the *Kars for Kids* jingle – that song can get stuck for hours and days.

Just as folks say, and it is true that you "can't unsee some things." Those are the kinds of things that get trapped in your mind—the things you can't unsee or unhear.

Some secular music is that way and that is because that music has been prayed over by 30 or more witches so that it will be popular, liked and played and played by those who hear it; that music is demonically anointed. Songs are enchanted over, not for the sake of the song, but for the sake of capitalism. They call it praying, but it's witches so it is enchantment.

In this way when a witch incants, that is enchants over words (with or without music) they are very susceptible to get stuck in your mind.

People love to interpret this as the imaginations being your own thoughts, your own ideas, and maybe they are because a lot of our self-talk can be negative. Know this, whatever thoughts you are being fed come from the idols or demons in your soul, and what has been *sent* to you. So, if you welcome them, house them, they will sit down and chat you up. Deliverance is needed and you can do it yourself by resisting them and repenting and renouncing whatever you did to open the door for them in the first place. But most people don't know what they did to invite in demons.

I read somewhere years ago, that to cancel a negative thought open your mouth and speak what God says instead of what the negative thought is. They say you need to speak the positive 10 times to negate and cancel that one negative or evil thought. So do that.

Don't fire a cannon at yourself with powerful spiritual weapons, just speak the Word of God over your life to counter an evil thought.

You also can't just *think* the opposite, you've got to say it out loud because faith comes by hearing. You can't just listen to someone else say it, although you may frame what you are going to say by hearing what the other person said, as long as it is of God. Then you've got to speak and say it, pray it, decree it, declare it and **believe** it! Then receive what God says not what some uninformed or evil person says about you.

What about the negative things being said about you **that you don't even hear**--, in the natural? Those things are being said whether you hear them or not. If you hear them and do nothing that is worse than not hearing them. However, not hearing them doesn't negate them. This is why you spend time in the Word, and in praise & Worship and speak the Word over yourself. Some well-meaning people may blindly curse another, or some evil person may be up all night sending curses to others. The Word of God is your counter to all of that.

At the start I said that evil imaginations are the work of witches, warlocks, wizards, the demonic and the occultic. What if someone is enchanting against you? What if they are standing behind you and enchanting against you, or seeking information on you from a *familiar spirit*, an ancestral power, or other evil altar? What if this is happening in church, and you think nothing of it because you are in church, and people don't do bad things in church. Oh, yes they do. Even good-looking people can do awful things in churches.

Voices

Who are you listening to? Of course I can say it fancy: *to whom are you listening?*

We're taking an overview of the entire Book of Job. We will focus on a few points that the Lord has shared with me that I want to share with you.

Job seems to me a whole lesson on witchcraft or devil-craft. Job is the poster child for undeserved suffering. In this life, we go through things that we wonder, *why is this happening to me? What has happened here?* We are sometimes shocked and believe that what is happening is undeserved and unfair.

Job had a lot of wealth. Job served God. Job had a hedge of protection about him. Job had 10 kids, and they partied kind of hardy. Job made regular sacrifices to God for his kids just in case the kids had sinned. He sent up sacrifices for them to God, so he and the whole family would be in good standing with Jehovah.

But Satan, the accuser of the brethren, got permission to attack Job. In the Book of Deuteronomy 28 we are told clearly starting at about verse 15, what the Curse of the Law is and what these curses are. Job was a man blameless and upright, and one who feared God and shunned evil. God described Job to Satan: have you considered my servant Job? He is upright; there is none like him on the Earth. He is a blameless man.

I don't blame God here because people with children like to brag on their kids. I'd like to be a kid that God brags on, wouldn't you?

God describes Job again in Chapter 2 because Satan had already gotten permission to do things to Job and God is still bragging on Job. Job, in my opinion, is a forerunner, a type and shadow of Jesus who was in Heaven, in a lot of wealth, serving God. But then Jesus came to Earth and became poor, just as Job was experiencing lack after he had enjoyed a lot of wealth because when Satan attacked him, he really hit him in his wallet.

Jesus served God exclusively. And there was a hedge of protection about Jesus as well. So this is how I'm comparing Jesus and Job. Jesus was up in the Third Heaven, but He came to Earth for our sakes. And He came here and became poor, relatively poor compared to what He had been living in. Jesus also was not a sinner, but he *became* sin.

Then Jesus was persecuted by powers of evil; just about everywhere He went there was opposition, somebody just waiting to confront Jesus when He was doing His ministry. Jesus hadn't really done anything to them; He came here to help them, not to hurt them. But Jesus took sin upon Himself for those whom He loved--, us.

Job couldn't have been touched by Satan, that is, without God's permission. And Jesus never could have been crucified without God's permission. God had set this thing up. Job in a real sense was a hero, a forerunner, and a type in shadow, as said.

Satan confronted, tormented, and tortured Job to see if Job would curse God, at least that was his excuse. During 42 chapters of attack and torment, Job did fall into the flesh, but he did not curse God.

Since Satan had done this to Job, he thought he could do this to any man, and every man. So, he still accuses the brethren in evil petition to get judgments to attack mankind.

However, because of Jesus's work at Calvary, because of His death, burial, and resurrection, we have a stronger protection from that same thing happening to us, although the accuser will present Evil Petitions at the Courts of Heaven to get a judgment on a man, any man, any woman. Unless we give the Accuser an open door by disobedience, rebellion, or sin we have our Stronghold, the Strong Tower of the Lord as our protection.

Jesus, at first, asked that the Cup of the Cross pass from Him, but then He acquiesced and willingly gave into the plan of God for man's Salvation. In that resolution to go to the Cross Satan then had the right to attack and torment Jesus--, but he didn't and could not **kill** Jesus.

Of course, the devil believed he had defeated Jesus and won over God, but he didn't, has not, and will not. Jesus gave up the Ghost, He was **not killed**.

WE WIN

Jesus could have called 12 legions of Angels at any time and especially to come down off that Cross. A legion is just about 6000, so 12 legions is 72,000. Jesus could have called 72,000 Angels at any time. That Cross was an Altar and altars require sacrifices. The Sacrifice above sacrifices cannot be undone or triumphed over.

In the heat of a battle, when the evil king in the Old Testament sacrificed his own son on the wall, even God had to honor that for power and victory, even against God's own people, (2 Kings 3:27).

You want victory? What are you sacrificing? Nothing? Well, that's why your results are so abysmal.

The Voice of the Spirit

But the plan was for the redemption of man back to God. The plan was to save and deliver a sin sick world. And because Jesus listened to the Voice of the Spirit of God. He listened to the right Voice; therefore we are safe and we are thankful.

Jesus often had angels around Him. He had an Angel that strengthened Him in Gethsemane before He went to the Cross. And while He was hanging on the Cross, He could have come down. He could have gotten down from that Cross. But He had you on His mind He had me on His mind, so He stayed up there for the redemption of a sin sick world, for redemption of mankind.

But Satan kept on with his plan that he had. He wants to keep doing evil in the Earth. Satan gets people in the Earth to do bad things.

He gets people to do evil for him. A lot of the time he is deceiving people, but many *want* to do evil. That's who they are; those are they who listen to the voice of the devil.

Remember 1/3 of the angels fell with Satan. They are *spirits*, and have no body in the Earth, so they recruit, buy (and sell) souls, overtake bodies and trick people into giving their authority over to the devil. But he gives false promises, counterfeit promises, wealth, fame, power, whatever they really want to hear. He offers them stuff that they are lusting for. They want it now, they want it fast, they want it yesterday.

So, there are these people who want power. They think they have a special gift? Many think, special family powers that they've inherited from grandma, grandpa--, somebody. You can inherit demons down your family line, but no one inherits the Holy Spirit. Real Wisdom and knowledge and gifts are given by the Holy Spirit, not by grandma or grandpa. Some of these special folks want to conjure up and try to control demons. People, you cannot control demons. Some of the demons that fell when Lucifer was kicked out of Heaven don't even obey him, so what do you think you're going to do?

Some think they can make nice with demons and say some magic words or something to get these demons to do things for them, including stuff against other people. That's another whole lesson. It's like they have never even heard of a *quid pro quo*. You know, where the devil's gonna want something in return from that conjurer? And usually, it's way more than the conjurer wants to pay? Usually, it's everything.

If God allowed Job to be tested perhaps there was some *household* evil in Job's world.. God doesn't break His own laws or statutes. Household witchcraft may be what allowed the devil to do evil to Job, because there was a way for the devil to get in. There was a problem in Job's household, possibly unhealed ancestral open doors. And because this verse in Job, says that Job was upright and blameless, that it must not have been Job.

Job was giving offerings for his kids. Were the kids even doing their own offerings? They must have been old enough to do so; they were grown-up enough to get together and have parties. Job was standing in the gap for those kids. Or it could have been unhealed ancestral doors that let the attacks in to Job and his family.

because a curse causeless will not alight. (Proverbs 26:2)

So, the devil comes in, and attacks Job's oxen, and sheep, his money, wealth, resources, and cash flow. But God sees that Job still didn't curse Him even after the devil did this.

The next thing the devil attacks Job's whole family, that's his legacy, his future. All of his kids are now dead--, by a great wind. Yet, Job says, *Naked came I out of my mother's womb. Blessed be the name of the Lord.* Then Job falls down on his face, and he worships God.

Then the devil wants to do more, so he goes back before the Throne of God with another Evil Petition. Now he gets permission to attack Job's body, but he is told not to kill Job.

Since the devil got permission, we might think there was somebody in Job's family who was under judgment. Or, there an ancestral sin, iniquity, or something that opened the door for Satan. The devil sends fever and boils but Job still didn't curse God.

Well, I wasn't there, but there is only one person in Job's family that wasn't hurt in all of the devil's attacks. That person may have been a *monitoring spirit*, or more, and the devil found her useful and did her no harm. That was Job's wife.

The First Attack

Hold it! When it comes to demonic attack, the first thing the devil attacked was Job's wealth, money, cash flow, and finances. So many people are under attack in just that very way by the devil. Job tears his robe, shaves his head and falls to the ground and worships God.

When there is enemy attack the first thing you must consider is your worship may not be right with the one you serve. You should be serving Jehovah God, so like Job, re-up your worship and fall down and worship the Lord.

Idol *gods* rage and rampage when they are not getting worship. If you are saved, and in Christ you should only be worshipping the Lord, so upgrade your worship to the Lord, making it clear that you serve no other gods. The Lord does not deserve shabby worship.

Seven Days & Nights

Next, here comes Job's three friends, Eliphaz, Bildad and Zophar. Job's grief was so great that for seven days and for seven nights, no one spoke. You know these were men. Seven days and seven nights no one spoke; you know these were not women.

If no one spoke for these seven days and seven nights, and they weren't having a prayer vigil. Then each one was just listening. Listening to whoever they listen to. Whomever they hear within themselves. If you ask a man what he is thinking, he can quickly say, *Nothing*. But, I believe thoughts are broadcast to men and women all day long.

What were these four silent men *hearing*? Were they listening to their own flesh? How they're feeling over there with Job? Are they listening to their souls, how their emotions are and how their intellect thinks the problem with Job is. Were they in their flesh, observing by sight what Job is looking like. Were they obeying their will? Do they want to stay because that's what *friends* do, and they were concerned about their own reputations? Did they stay and just keep looking at Job watching him suffer or do they really want to leave and get back to their own comforts? Who are they really listening to? Are they listening to God? Are they listening to their own spirit man? Are they listening to the Spirit of God?

Who do you listen to?

So, Job ended up cursing the day, but he didn't curse God. But it does come to light that Job was in fear and that is an open door. Fear is an open door. Job said the things that he greatly feared had come upon him. Fear and other sins open the door for bad things to happen. With spiritual amnesia we somehow play innocent, stating or believing that we're not the blame for **anything** that happens to us, even when we're under assault by the devil, by devil craft known as witchcraft.

A household witch can easily open the door for the devil to invade or attack the house and sell out one or all of a family if that family is not properly serving God.

We all had better know who we are related to and who is allowed into our house and personal space.

Here are some of the things that may be happening when devil craft arrives. It is a short list, but it is why I say that Job is a lesson in witchcraft attack.

The attacked person will become disoriented and confused.

He may start to question God. He may question his own spirituality. He may question his own relationship with God, and question how God is dealing with him, feeling unfairly treated or even persecuted. He may question his own being, even asking, *Why is he here?*

Even Sicker

When a person is targeted by curses, he becomes emotionally and/or physically drained as Job probably was. There is a darkness or cloud over their face. His friends said they didn't even recognize Job because he looked so bad when they saw him.

The back of the victim's neck is tight. It feels like there is a band around their head like a bizarre but intense migraine. The person will think they're sick physically--, they are, but this is not normal, physiological sickness. This person is **sick by witchcraft**.

In order for the curse to alight there has to be a cause. Once the witch finds out the *cause*, the sin, the iniquity in the person they want to attack they've identified the person's sin sickness. Now like a demonic nurse or doctor they know where and how it hurts, now they can make it hurt worse; they can make their victim even sicker.

Yes, I'm saying the sinner is already sick and either spiritually dead or on the way there; the witch by witchcraft, the devil, by devil craft tightens the screw and makes that sinner even sicker.

With a heart of compassion when Jesus sees us sick in our sin, He comes to rescue us. When the devil sees us sick in our own sin, he comes in for the kill. If not the kill, to further manipulate the situation for his own benefit which includes getting the compromised, desperate person to do something even worse than what they've already done. This something may then affect one or many others. And, also the devil wants man to do wrong so he can accuse that man and win an evil petition against him, and also so he can embarrass God.

Fear begins to plague the mind. And then there's the imaginations. Gross imaginations flood the mind. The imaginations cast into the mind, or created by the attacks that have been sent to an individual are the imaginations that need to be cast down, struck down, even shot down.

Depending on how this person handles himself and the normal sequela of devil craft attack, such as a lack of sound restful, deep sleep at the proper intervals, this person could spiral down quickly. You go to sleep, but you wake up exhausted, wondering, *Why was I in bed if I'm still exhausted?* All of a sudden, your peace is gone. You can't stay asleep, even if you do fall asleep.

There are pains in your body, sometimes they are vague, and you can't even describe them to a doctor. Even if you do, no doctor can find anything wrong with you. You are not physically sick; you are **witchcraft sick.**

That does not mean that you should go to a witch doctor. Never do that.

You may feel discouraged, depressed, defeated, hopeless, dissatisfied. Spiritual life is dried up. You just generally feel achy, the stiff neck, back, heavy shoulders, heaviness on the chest, having sharp pains out of nowhere, buzzing in your ears, sometimes outbreaks in your skin. The fever and the boils Job had is all part of the witchcraft attack to include physical fatigue – low energy.

Then there's the clumsiness--, bumping into things, and things bumping into you. Accidents. Falling. Fender benders. Sprained ankles. Little cuts, scrapes, tears, bruises. You're a mess.

You start to question your spirituality, and even your spiritual leaders. The devil wants to separate you from spiritual support, help, growth, and especially deliverance. You may start to backslide. Past hurts come up--often. You may feel rejected, lonely. No one understands you. You feel you're the only one who's going *through*. Confusion, doubt, forgetfulness, sudden attacks of dizziness, series of tragedies. Your business falls off. Remember, the first thing Job lost was his finances. It was all gone. It doesn't take all of these symptoms, any combination can indicate witchcraft attack.

Be sure you pray and ask God what is going on with you. He will show you. And, He will also show you the source, not for a physical fight, but for spiritual warfare.

Suddenly you feel *different*, but you don't know why. There are arguments--, you're arguing with everybody, but you don't know why. There are tormenting dreams, food in the dreams, sex in the dream. Some people even have marks on their bodies when they wake up and they were alone in bed, and they know they didn't scratch themselves.

This is witchcraft attack.

- Back to sender, in the Name of Jesus.

Witchcraft works like this: The devil or his agent does something, even a little something, and the results of what was done to their victim gets into this person's body and head. Then, the person, depending on who they are listening to in their life, will respond in pretty predictable ways. Their response is usually as devastating as the attack itself.

- **Lord, save me from myself, in the Name of Jesus.**

Are they listening to their flesh?? Then watch, and the flesh will do the rest of the damage. The flesh cannot cast down an imagination.

Are they listening to their soul? They'll go into their emotions. They'll go into their own intellect. They lean to their own understanding or their own will and become stubborn. They may stop praying, stop going to church, stop listening to Wisdom and stop going to God, often leaving themselves open to do the rest of the damage to themselves.

The victims of witchcraft become weary of going *through*; it is a game of attrition. If you are flesh and blood fighting a *spirit* (demon) that doesn't fatigue as a man does, who do you think will win a war of attrition? If you're not going to God, reading the Word, and in spiritual warfare the enemy that is a *spirit* will not be weakened. It'll wear you down, if you're not fighting back. In God, in prayers is how you counter this attack.

A jealous person or a jealous adversary is very dangerous. The *spirit* of jealousy impregnates the fight, and it is a *spirit*, unending, with too much energy. The devil is jealous of your relationship with God. He cannot be redeemed, but mankind can. A jealous person or an intensely jealous person usually wants to hurt you, delay you, stall you, stop you, bankrupt you. sometimes they even want you gone from the face of the Earth. A witch is not a cute or sexy Halloween costume; witches are under the same mandate as their boss, Satan. A witch's assignment is to steal, kill, and destroy.

What you must do in witchcraft attack is not what you would naturally do; the enemy has anticipated that. You must have a Christ-like response, else the curse or spell sticks and will escalate predictably. The only way you can have a Christ-like response to something that your soul and flesh would rise up and take over to "help" you is to have your soul and flesh completely under subjection of the Holy Spirit. Completely. You must be completely in Christ--, all in. Christ in you, you in Christ, the hope of Glory. It is the glory of victory when you defeat the evil arrows and witchcraft, the devil craft that may come against you.

Job was under attack, he was acting like a normal human through many chapters, but soon he fell on his face and worshipped God. Then he sent up offerings and worshipped God. Then Job prayed for his friends and he, himself was delivered. Those are Godly responses while going through; the natural, carnal man will not do that.

That Christ-like response is a response your enemy can't withstand (resist). The Fruit of the Spirit as you recall, the Word says, *Against such there is no law.* Grace, which God gives us as we are going through is a power and it is greater than the law. Love is the greatest of all.

There is no spell, hex, vex, or incantation that came defeat Christ or Christ-likeness. Whatever fine print and evil code is embedded in a curse, even if it anticipated a man responding any other way than a natural man, there is nothing greater than what Jesus would do. The standard that Jesus raises just by being Jesus and doing what He would do abates any flood of the enemy.

But, how will you know what to do?

In Your Mind

You must listen to your spirit man. You have to build up your spirit man, or else your spirit man becomes something foreign to you, and you'll hear people say things like, *Something told me, Something said*, or *Something told me to go this way instead of that way.*

What was that *something*? That something was the who was that we listen to. Ideally, it should be the Holy Spirit giving guidance and direction to your spirit, the spirit of man.

I count a minimum of five voices that could be talking to you at any given time. You have got to know that five *voices* all with equal opportunity to speak is confusion. I am not talking about audible voices that you hear in the natural indicating that you're having some kind of a psychotic split. I speak of an inner unction, an inkling, a nudging--, that's what I mean by *voices*.

Most confused people are listening to many voices. They have many idols or demons in their ear, in their soul telling them many different things, most all of them lies. Hopefully you're listening to the Holy Spirit of God, if not at least you should be listening to your own spirit, the spirit of man, the spirit that God has given to us.

If not, you may be listening to your emotions, your will, and your intellect in your soul. Or worse, you could be listening to your flesh; all these have a voice and may hold sway over a person. Of your five senses the *voice* of your sight may want to be in charge of your life. Most people just believe what they see. Or the *voice* of what you hear wants to be in control because faith comes by hearing. Sometimes people will tell you things that are not true, and you may gain faith for it whereas you should not. You need to apply the Word of God to everything. Pray to God, ask Him, *Is this truth? Is it real? Do I act on this?*

Then there's the voice of your touch. People say, *I know because I was there.* There is the voice of your smell; something may not smell right to you. it might smell fishy, wrong, or suspicious. Sometimes it may not smell funny or off. There is a possibility to miss the whole thing because the devil can put a pleasant aroma over a really stinky situation and hide it under something that smells sweet. One of the latest occultic tricks by occultic "pastors" is to use, sell, or give enchanted fragrances. Be careful and prayerful of everything you wear, use, bring into your home, and even inhale by smelling.

Then there is the *voice* of your taste. What does it taste like? Does it taste like something you've done before? Does it taste like something you've had before? Do you know this? You may say within yourself, I want to taste something, so I want to do something *different*. A taste of sin is very dangerous because the flesh will probably like it, and the flesh likes to repeat what it likes. The flesh is subject to addiction.

For I know that in me (that is, in my flesh,) dwelleth no good thing: for to will is present with me; but how to perform that which is good I find not. (Romans 7:18)

Then, there's the voice of the Devil. Don't think that the devil has some ugly hideous voice. Satan was Lucifer who was built and assigned as the worship leader in Heaven. What kind of voice do you think he may have? If you think that all fallen angels lost all their power when they were cast out of Heaven, think again. The devil's voice is probably lovely and mellifluous--, or *can* be. Not only can he use that voice to deceive people, he can anoint the voices of others (who ask him) to deceive others as well. Even though we are talking about voices, the devil has the ability to anoint eyes, smiles--, anything that he may use to ensnare men into sin. Proverbs warns the young man to not let an evil woman entice you with her "eyelids." Beauty is only skin deep, especially if you don't know the source of that beauty, or that *voice*.

They say that those from the evil marine kingdom can present as especially beautiful; it's part of their enchantment. Additionally, folklore has spoken for ages about mermaids, mermen, and sirens. Sirens are known because of their song to draw and entrap a man--, their voice then is demonically anointed.

The devil's trying to make you feel good. He wants you to believe that he will give you satisfaction. He wants to make you feel okay, or justified, or you're right to do what you just did, because you *feel* like it in your flesh. Your flesh is satisfied that you just did something to somebody or just told somebody off or cussed somebody out. Man often thinks that he will get soul or spirit satisfaction from a flesh act, but he is tricked because flesh satisfaction does not convert to satisfaction for the other aspects of your being.

Or the devil will prod at your will convincing you to be stubborn, rebellious, insubordinate or disrespectful, so when you sin, he can enter into and control a soul.

The devil may prod at your intellect; now I say, *Hello, Left Brains.*

A lot of people are really intelligent and blessed with smarts from God; these are the left brained people. If a left-brained person can't figure a thing out in their head, if they can't wrap their minds around it, then there will be a challenge getting them to really understand things of the Spirit or to follow the Lord. God chooses the foolish things to confound the wise.

That means that you've to use your spirit man to understand God. And that's why Jesus spoke in parables, because everything He was saying was not for everyone. What Jesus was talking about was discerned and understood by the Spirit of God; Jesus' haters didn't have the Spirit of God with them, and that's why they hated Him. They did not know Him. After that, the Spirit of God flows into and ministers to the spirit of man. The things of God are not understood by the mind of a man.

However, the spirit of the man is also what operates the smarts of a man, the smart part of the brain, the critical thinking part of the brain. So, your spirit man has to be built up to understand spiritual things.

God talks to man by man's spirit, not by man's five senses necessarily or by his emotions, or intellect, exclusively.

Feelings

Speaking of renting rooms in your head, the devil may check into your emotions, and this one is huge. Many people completely run their lives by emotions. It's all about *feel*, how they feel emotionally about this or that as to whether they will do or don't do a thing. Whether they'll say a thing or stop talking altogether.

And the devil really touched the emotions of Job when he killed all of Job's kids in the same day.

By Chapter 10 God can see that Job is really depressed. But it is the spirit of a man that will sustain him in trouble; depression is certainly trouble. The spirit of man is grown up and shored up by the Holy Spirit of God.

More about this in my book series *Upgrade: How to Get Out of Survival Mode.*

The Garments

When devil craft, or witchcraft attacks come, we all have to figure out if we did anything to open the door. *Why is this happening to me? Am I under judgment from God*? Or, Is God doing something supernatural and amazing and prophetic and futuristic in our lives that causes us or calls for us to have to share sin the sufferings of Jesus?

In Him we move and breathe and have our being. But by Chapter 10, Job was depressed, and then he begins talking. Now Job will begin to listen to his own voice; will it be the voice of his spirit man, his soul and emotions, or of his flesh? Job begins talking about the moth-eaten garment that he is now wearing, and that his *garments* have been changed.

He was wearing spiritual garments of respect and dignity before. By chapter 16, all the stuff that the devil has done to Job clearly shows him that his life has been downgraded. However, he was assigning it to God because he doesn't realize that the devil has done this to him,

Which is more of the lesson on witchcraft. People who practice it like to do things to you and still be your *friend* and will even smile in your face. That's the fun of it, to them. While they're doing things to you and tricking you, you don't even suspect that it's them, unless you're praying to God and allowing God to talk to you by your spirit, because Spirit will tell you things, even lead you into all Truth.

Also, God tells you things by the dream.

Job knew something was happening that was spiritual, so he assigned these calamities to God. He didn't realize that it was the devil doing all of this. We need to be discerning enough not to do that even now. It is blasphemy to assign evil that the devil has done blaming it on God. As well, it is blasphemy to give the devil credit for the good that God has done. Don't get on a slippery slope, folks.

So, it depends on what *voice* you are listening to. Which *voice* you are listening to is also is which **hand** is moving things in your life. It is a hard lesson, but we need to know this.

By Chapter 16, verse 11 Job says, *God has delivered me to the ungodly and turned me over into the hands of the wicked.* He realizes what's happening is wicked.

When you're going through, where are your friends? Job had three friends who came to his house, but they didn't have anything to say for seven days. I hope they were praying. But at least Job's friends were there. Where are your friends, especially when you're going *through*? Are they of value to you? Are they real friends?

Do you have natural support in this life? Do you have spiritual support? Do you have emotional support?

If you answered yes to those questions, then you have friends, real friends. If you're always considered the strong one and you are always giving out support, who is pouring back into your life? You need to know a friend when you see one, be a friend, and keep a friend for these kinds of support in your life.

If you have no friends, there is Jesus Christ who sticks closer than a brother, but a person needs people in the natural reflecting Christ to him, as well. If you are surrounded by users who only take and don't give, you are a candidate for many kinds of attacks.

Elihu

Elihu is the *comforter* of Job. He is younger than the three friends, and younger than Job. So, he's trying to be respectful, but he kind of comes off as, *I wasn't gonna say anything, but he had to.*

Elihu was not going to say anything, but since he couldn't find any real Wisdom in what these older men were saying, Elihu had to speak up. He ended up saying that Job's reaction to Job's calamity was sinful. And Elihu suggested that Job should recognize his suffering as a discipline of God that will lead to a reconciliation with God.

The LORD hath chastened me sore: but he hath not given me over unto death, (Psalm 118:18)

Elihu said that Job had added rebellion to his sin, and he clappeth his hands among us, and multiplied his words against God.

Don't you know that most of the stuff that the cool people say is in the Bible and came out of the Bible? Job **clapped his** hands. Listen to me when I talk, when people are really trying to be emphatic, that's what they do nowadays. That was in the Bible. Without God, you're not doing anything new; there is nothing new under the sun. **But we don't dare- Clap. Our. Hands. At. God.**

By this time, God is pretty much done with all of them. And he says, *You know what I said, I accept Job, but these three friends---,*

God got Job to do a sacrifice. He and his friends brought in some bullocks. Job priested and sent up an offering and prayed for his friends. This is when Job was re-established with God. Once he was re-established spiritually, all of his brothers and sisters, and acquaintances came and had a meal with Job. They consoled him and comforted him, and each one gave him a piece of silver and a ring of gold. Job got better than a Go-Fund-Me, he got a God-Fund-Me.

At first, Job was rejected by his family and friends, as if he were a spiritual pariah, but now he was accepted again. When one is wearing a bad garment in the spirit as Job had described, in the natural people will treat you differently, even unto reproach.

How could God let an innocent man, a righteous man experience such terrible suffering?

Job had fear. Job had accused God, and Job was self-righteous. Job was upright, but he wasn't perfect. Job was bitter, he became depressed and suicidal. All that fear was a counter to faith and love, showing that Job's confidence wasn't fully in God, but in Job's spiritual *works*.

But we are not saved by works, yet fulfilling the Law was what Old Testament man constantly ascribed to. It not until the New Testament that we learn no man is saved by works, but Salvation is the gift of God. We are saved by Grace. Thank You, Lord.

For by grace are ye saved through faith; and
that not of yourselves: it is the gift of God:
Not of works, lest any man should boast.
(Ephesians 2:8-9)

In his suffering, Job had accused God of being hostile and unfair to him and that God was the one aiming all this misfortune, tragedy, and calamity at him. But it wasn't God; it was the devil. He believed that God made him into a prisoner, but that was the devil. He believed that God was trying to kill him, but that was the devil.

How could God let an innocent man experience such terrible suffering?

My answer to that and by the revelation of the Spirit of God, is Jesus. Jesus was an innocent, just and perfect man who experienced terrible suffering for you and for me. Yet Jesus never accused God and was never self-righteous.

Matthew 27:19, Pilate's wife said, *I have nothing to do with that just man.* Pilate said in Matthew 27:24. *I'm innocent of the blood of this just person.*

One of the criminals on the Cross next to Jesus said, *This man has done nothing wrong,* (Luke 23:41). In Luke 23:47, the Centurion said, *Surely, this was a righteous man.*

As Jesus did, Job also suffered, but then he saved his friends--, not with the kind of salvation that Jesus has for us, but in his own way, as a prototype, a type and shadow of Jesus. Job saved his friends because God accepted Him and accepted His sacrifice.

Jesus saved us because God accepted His Sacrifice, that is He accepted Jesus. So, Jesus became sin for us.

Job offered the sacrifice for his friends, but Jesus offered the ultimate sacrifice for all His friends, and all that would become His friends. Jesus provided eternal life to us. Job, in intercession turned away God's wrath, as did Jesus turn away the wrath of God from mankind for all man's sins.

And so it was that after the Lord accepted Job's intercession, that God said to those three friends, *My wrath is aroused against you. For you have not spoken of me what is right as my servant Job has.*

Listen

God did not treat Job's friends according to their foolishness, and their folly, and they didn't receive the punishment they deserved. Neither has God treated us according to our disobedience, rebellion, sin, foolishness, folly. But we have avoided God's judgment because Jesus interceded for us, Our Great Intercessor. And we are still avoiding the punishment we really deserve because of Grace --, we are under the Dispensation of Grace right now, but we need to get it right.

Teach me what I cannot see;
if I have done wrong, I will not do so again.
(Job 34:32)

When the Teacher is teaching, the student must hear and learn. Listen to the Word of the Lord. Listen to the Spirit of the Lord. Listen to whom God sends. Listen to His Prophets, His pastors, His teachers, the Prayer warriors, listen to the Watchmen on the walls, listen to the intercessors.

Listen to God because Jesus has released the Holy Spirit to the Earth, to be our helper, our intercessor, Our Guide, and our Paraclete.

Listen, to build up your spirit man. Listen to Him, (Proverbs 18:14).

The spirit of man can save your life. Who are you listening to? Whomever you are listening to, you are learning from, whether you intend to or not.

Let your soul prosper and possess it in honor, but the spirit is supposed to be running your life. You need to keep your flesh under the subjection of the Spirit. You listen by keeping under the subjection of the Holy Spirit. (1 Corinthians 9:27); this is who you listen to for a victorious life in Christ.

In this Dispensation of Grace, we would do well to grow and build up our spirit man, so we will listen to the right *voice*. Do the right things for our life, our godliness for ministry, for our family, for our purpose, for Destiny and for Your Glory, Lord, in the Name of Jesus.

Five Voices

Who are *you* listening to?

Job had a lot of undeserved suffering. Attacked in his money, in his family and even in his flesh. Job's symptoms perfectly mirrored witchcraft, devil craft attacks.

Job worshipped, communed with God, listened to God. The devil jumped in and attacked Job. Under attack, Job went into his flesh, and deteriorated into soulish talk and soulish speak, but he did not curse God.

Job's wife listened to the voice of her flesh throughout and spoke out of the voice of her flesh. Whatever people are listening to, their mental talk--- that's what they will speak. By people's actions and what they repeat we will know what they are listening to in their inner being.

Job's friends were listening to a combo of emotions and flesh.

Elihu, I believe listened to Wisdom, one of the seven Spirits around the Throne of God.

The Spirit of the Lord will rest on Him,
(Isaiah 11:2).

I Wisdom was with the Lord when He began His work... even before the world began.
(Proverbs 8:22)

There are *at least* five voices that any of us can be influenced by any time, day or night.

- Holy Spirit
- Spirit of man
- Your soul
- Your flesh
- The devil

Job says there is a spirit of man and the inspiration of the Almighty.

If we listen, when our spirit is being ministered to by the Holy Spirit of God, then we will receive Wisdom like Elihu. Wisdom, instruction, knowledge, and understanding cause us to make better decisions in our life to live a godly life, a better life.

Then there is the voice of the soul which include your will and your intellect. And, thirdly from your soul, are your emotions. Collectively your soul has a *voice*, but each component has sit's own input, and is certainly vying for top position.

Your flesh has five senses: sight, hearing, touch, smell, and taste. And they each have a *voice* within that *voice*, but I speak collectively. The *voice* of your flesh speaks loudly, maybe too loudly.

Worst of all, there's the voice of the devil, who will try to sell you anything, talk you into anything and talk you out of everything. The most base aspect of man's being is his flesh. The serpent is the most base of animals, crawling on the ground. He's low level so he tempts the flesh, which is low hanging fruit, easy to reach, often. But he also antagonizes the soul and spirit of a man if he can.

Man is a very complex being--, fearfully and wonderfully made. There's no way we can think we don't need God. How can we actually understand ourselves except to ask the One who made us? It takes a wise person to finally realize that you really don't know much of anything, and other than not knowing that, you don't know what you're doing, unless you read the Bible, the manual for your life.

If we don't know that we need order and structure in our lives, then, I'm not really sure what any of us are doing. As we're picking someone to be the lead of our life, to be the Lord of our life, to be the supreme being of our life, that would be God. If we're picking somebody, we're gonna pick the best person. Well, the best person is not your flesh. The best voice is not your flesh. The best voice is definitely not the devil. The best voice is not your soul. Even though there's some smarts in there, it's not the best voice to listen to run your life.

The best *could* be your own spirit, and sometimes you do incline to your own spirit, but mostly it is the **Holy Spirit** that is the best and the smartest. Of the voices which is the wisest one? The calmest one? The most powerful one? The one with the best track record?

It is definitely the Holy Spirit. You have the Holy Spirit, right? You know how to hear the Holy Spirit, yes? The Holy Spirit speaks of God, so ultimately God is the best one.

Compared to God, we're all just babies. We don't know things. Don't get caught in the old devil trap where someone by a *familiar spirit* tells you your past – any demon knows your past. We need to be progressive, not regressive. We need God, He knows what's ahead of us. He knows where we are right now. He knows what we need. He knows the decisions that we make now will impact us in the future? We need God. So, people of God and *future* people of God, you need God. Hallelujah. We also need to know which *voice* we are really listening to.

Our Pickers

We get spiritual impulses and spiritual influences all through our daily lives, but just because something is spiritual doesn't mean it is God. You have to know that you know that it's God.

The devil is also trying to communicate to our spirit man to influence evil in us. We must know the difference in all these voices, so we are not deceived.

God has gifted us. God has given us lots of blessings. Thank You, Lord. Some of us are really smart. We have high intelligence. We can learn and retain things very well. Some of us are excellent at critical thinking.

However, some of us, they say, couldn't think our way out of a paper bag. Even worse, there are some that couldn't even think their way through air. I mean, really, do you go left? Do you go right? Do you go straight ahead? We need God.

Ladies, some of us may find it confusing if we've got two guys who are trying to talk to us. Two suitors, two guys that want to date us and we need to pick *one*. I'm sorry to say, if you have a broken **picker**, you don't know how to pick a guy. Or maybe you didn't even know you had a **picker**. But you do.

Your picker is your choice maker. Your picker is your decider, and you need it, and you use it all day long. What's for breakfast? What's for lunch? What's the best route to take to work? Which melon is the right melon at the market? Where do you park your car? You pick. You decide. You choose. All day long and all night long. Yep, even in your sleep, even in your dreams. You're picking.

In Deuteronomy 28, we *choose* all day long. We choose the Word says. God says choose this day. Who you gonna serve. That means you need a picker. You need to choose. It is a very famous passage and God gives us free will, so we can choose. We choose.

But back to this romantic question. If a guy is presented with the same question if, say, they're two ladies, they're interested in him, well, which woman? Let's put it this way, if you've got a broken *picker*, or if your *picker* is out of commission, you may ask somebody else.

Or women, you may ask somebody. You may ask your angry brother or your jealous girlfriend to pick for you. You may ask your mother or your father. Know this, the person who helps you pick will tell you based on the *voice* that they're listening to. Whoever they're listening to, whatever *voice* they're listening to, or whoever they hear the most, that's the advice they're gonna give you. The angry brother, the jealous girlfriend are both listening to either the devil or their flesh, or both.

The *voice* a person hears and listens to the most is the trusted voice that guides their decisions. Others will be influenced by what influences them, and they will influence you by what influences them, sometimes whether you ask or not--, but especially if you ask.

Man, when it comes to picking who you want to date if there is a choice of two ladies, too often he will pick both ladies. (Or try to.)

If *more* than two women want to date a man, sometimes they'll try to pick all of the women. And a man may think this is fun, or they may think it's funny, or they may think they're popular. It's probably because they don't know what whoredoms is. Maybe they don't know what polygamy is? Maybe they do, and just don't care, thinking that nothing will happen to them, they've just been elected king of a household or two, where they have no right to be *king*.

It's not fun or funny to the person who thinks they're the only woman, but there are more women that they're competing against, and they didn't even know it. Men, in cases like this, your friends may cheer you on, they may celebrate you, but you are just bringing on a world of hurt to yourself.

There will be lamentation later. Trust that. Because you're out there, in the streets, and you really don't need to hurt yourself that way. And you don't really need to hurt anybody else with your **broken *picker***.

Didn't you read the directions at the beginning of the Book of Deuteronomy 28? God says choose you this day. Choose. Choose one. He didn't say choose all and every. He didn't say you can choose to serve God and the devil because a man cannot serve two masters. He will love one and will hate the other.

So, a person who doesn't **pick** God automatically chooses the devil.

A woman who can't pick, who's gotta get somebody to help her pick, and this man who can't pick because he wants everything--, both of those have defective *pickers*. When you should pick one, but you can't, perhaps that's an error in critical thinking. Maybe you're failing a test because you have character issues, and you can't pick **one**. Or maybe it's just an error that you didn't ask God. Because really, if you can't pick. Lord, you know.

Just let the Lord pick for you. I bring you King Solomon. Solomon and all of his women.

Yes, I'm challenging that he couldn't pick because Solomon had 1000 wives and concubines, but he only had three children. So it kind of looks like those other 997 women married Solomon because of his status, and for his money. He had plenty of money. Why did Solomon marry them if not for children? Jacob had four wives, but he had 13 children. By that math, Solomon should have had 3,250 children.

Solomon seemed to have listened at that time to the *voice* of his flesh, even though Solomon was full of Wisdom and should have been listening to Wisdom, which means listening to the Spirit. Or Solomon could have been listening to the *voice* of his flesh, or the voice of whomever was advising him.

I don't know how many people were in Solomon's "kingdom" but of note is that *territorial spirits* want to marry all the women in that territory. If Solomon was listening to territorial demons, then he was then listening to the voice of the devil because that's who is ruling territories worldwide. And, it seems Solomon wanted to marry all the women in the territory, or every woman he saw.

Kings and people in high authority a lot of times have advisors, as they should. He could have been listening to the flesh of the advisor that was advising him. Solomon had asked God for Wisdom to rule God's people. Maybe Solomon should have asked God for Wisdom also for himself, so he'd have a good ***picker***.

Adam and Eve in the Garden of Eden had a choice. The choice was every other tree in the garden or the one tree that you're not supposed to eat from. This could have been an issue of *greed*. And they just wanted to eat from all the trees. They were probably listening to the *voice* of their flesh. *You know, that looks kind of good to eat. Eve, what's for dinner tonight? Let's eat tha*t.

Some people don't even want to make a decision. They don't want to decide. They don't want to *pick*. They want to get somebody else to decide for them so if it goes sideways, if it goes wrong, then guess what? Their ***Blamer*** works. I bet you their blamers are not broken. Folks will cast blame and throw shade quickly. Adam did it. He did it to God, saying, *God, that woman you gave me.* Adam didn't have to pick a wife, but he did use his picker to sin. Adam's picker was broken, but his blamer wasn't.

Picking is all too often a test of your soul's prosperity.

Off Screen

Have you seen this skit on social media where a child is given a treat. This food item is placed right in front of that kid, but he is not supposed to eat it until the caregiver, the parent gets back. Come on, it's a TikTok, so you know it's only a few seconds. The parents go off screen and we watch to see what the kid will do. This is a lesson in delayed gratification, and a gauge of soul prosperity.

Similarly, God went *off screen* with Adam and Eve and told them not to eat of that Tree. He turned his back for a moment, perhaps. And what did those two kids do in their Garden of Eden TikTok?

There is no one in the real TikTok telling the kids to go against what their parents had said. But the devil, with his voice said to Adam and Eve, *You're not gonna die if you eat from that tree.*

That was a lie, but he also didn't tell Adam he was going to get sick, really sick--, sin sick. He also didn't tell him that sin sickness would show up in Adam's soul, in Adam's body, and in their offspring. Sin Sickness leads to death. The Wages of Sin is Death, (Romans 6:23).

Nowhere in the Bible does it say that Adam and Eve got sick. But they did get sick; they got sin sick. And sin sickness is still a problem for all of mankind, all of the world today. Every unrepented sin leads to sin sickness of some sort, or the other.

The wages of sin is death. But right now, thank God, we do have the Better Blood. The Lord has given us remission from sin sickness, sickness of our body, and sickness of our wallets. He's redeemed us from death and from poverty. Hallelujah.

The Holy Spirit speaks to us, speaks to us by our Spirit man. He has influence. The Holy Spirit has a Voice. And our spirit, the spirit of man, has a *voice*. Our soul has a *voice*, our flesh has a *voice*, and of course, the devil has that voice that he has used on and against man for generations.

The spirit of man gives us inspiration. We've got the soul, which is the emotions, will and intellect, the flesh, which has sight, hearing, touch, smell, and taste.

Then there's the devil who can't be redeemed, but we can. He's jealous of our relationship with God. Can you imagine being in Heaven and getting kicked out, **forever**? Any of us may have been kicked out of worse places that you wanted to go back into.

Can you imagine Adam and Eve in the Garden of Eden, but then getting kicked out in Paradise? Lord, help us all. Imagine the best place you've ever been---, then you get put out and told never to return.

Eden is way better than that place. Heaven is way better than that place. The Presence of God is the best place to be. Don't sin, as much as it is in you, by help of the Holy Spirit. But, if you do, repent quickly. If you get defiled, pray immediately so you are not put out of the Presence of God. Ever.

More Than Five?

So, who are you listening to? Who are you listening to with your five (or more) *voices*? It depends on who you listen to the most. You train yourself to hear whom you want to spend time with. You train yourself to hear their voice and the stuff they would say. You train yourself to like it, really. And so you hear it more. You spend time with that voice. So, who have you listened to? The most of those five voices is going to be the one that you're going to let help you make decisions about things. And that's the one that's gonna become your *friend*.

John 15:15 says that the Lord is our friend, and we are so pleased that God would call us friend. But it's who you commune with, it's who you break bread with. If your soul is not prospered, you spend time with whomever you think will make you *happy*. Who or whatever's gonna say what you want to hear. Whoever's gonna give you what you want, whoever's gonna give you money, power, success, sex, whatever it is you think you're after, or whoever's gonna make life easy for you.

Who will present the least resistance to what your **flesh** really wants? That's who you will spend time with, that's who you're going to call, *friend*. But if you have a prospered soul, you will work diligently to build your soul up all the more. You will build up your spirit man and not your flesh.

The words that you trust in and rely on should be the Word of the Lord. If you have a prospered soul, you will continue building up your spirit man. You will come to know God as Father.

This passage says, I will declare the decree, the Lord hath said unto me, ***Thou art my son, this day I have begotten thee***.

Who wouldn't want to spend time with a loving father? So, God's words, are words that you can rely on because they're the words of Wisdom, words of Knowledge, words of Understanding, Counsel, and Might.

The *voice* of the Fruits of the Spirit, are joy and peace and patience and love and long-suffering, etcetera. There is the *voice* of the things that are lovely, the voice of the things that have good report, things that are true and have virtue.

Or perhaps you're just listening to yourself in your own echo chamber. You're your own person. Well then, what __*part*__ of yourself are you listening to? Man is fearfully and wonderfully made, but what part of yourself? Do you know? And do you really know the best thing or the best part of yourself to trust and rely on? Your flesh, your soul, or your spirit?

You've heard people say, *Oh, I just listen to my body*. Those are the people who listen to the voice of their flesh. If you are listening to your flesh, then you've got t break it down further; you have five senses; you should ask yourself which one is running the show?

In Adam and Eve's case, with their eyes they looked on the fruit and they decided it was good to eat. (Genesis), so that's sight and taste.

Our ears … (2 Kings 7:6)…

For the Lord hath made the host of the Syrians to hear a noise of Chariots and a noise of horses, even the noise of a great host. And they said, one to another, lo the king of Israel have hired us against us. The kings of the and the kings of the Egyptians to come upon us. And so then the hosts of the Assyrians, they fled.

The Syrians got out of there because. Their ears heard something that wasn't even there.

Then there's a sense of touch and taste and smell, as I said. Here were presented just a couple of examples of how the flesh can deceive you.

You must rely on the Lord. You need to rely on the Holy Spirit and the Word of Truth, the Word of God.

But then there's your soul. Your soul wants to run things, too. Your emotions, will, and intellect want to run your life.

Ultimately it is the Voice of God that is the most balanced, and the most knowledgeable and the most powerful. The danger is that faith comes by hearing, so when you hear the words of any other voices you could actually gain faith for what was said to you and act out that thing. Whoever you're listening to will feed your faith. Having faith for a thing deposits words and ideas and thoughts and influences into your heart. And then that Word becomes fully grown up and if you act on it, it could be a good thing if you've heard from the Lord. Or it could be a bad thing if it was the devil or some other *gray* thing in between. Depends on if it was your spirit, your soul, or your flesh.

The Quiet Voice

And he said, Go forth and stand upon the
mount before the Lord. And behold, the Lord
passed by, and a great and strong wind went
through the mountains, and breaking pieces,
the rocks before the Lord.

But the Lord was not in the wind, and after the
wind and earthquake of the Lord was not in the
earthquake and after the earthquake of fire, but
the Lord was not in the fire, and after the fire is
still small voice.

And it was so when Elijah heard it, that he
wrapped his face in his mantle, and went out,
and stood in the entering of The Cave. And
behold, there came a **voice** unto him, and said.
What doeth thou here, Elijah?
(1 Kings 19:11-13)

I repeat Verse 12.

And after the earthquake of fire, But the Lord
was not in the fire, And after the fire a still
small voice.

And you see, the voice of the Lord was in that voice. So, we must learn how to hear God. We must learn how to hear the Holy Spirit. And we must first recognize that the Holy Spirit is going to lead us back into all Truth and will lead us to God. He does not speak of Himself. He speaks of God. So first we recognize that God wants you sometimes to just sit down and be still. Be quiet, and He will speak to you in a still small voice.

It's not always about drama. God can be very dramatic because He's awesome like that, but He wants you to be still and know that He is God. And sometimes God does speak in that still, small *Voice*.

God's still, small Voice is the Voice of Mercy because in Psalms 29 says, *The voice of the Lord is over the waters, the God of glory thunders. The Lord thunders over the mighty waters. The voice of the Lord is powerful. The voice of the Lord is majestic. The voice of the Lord breaks the Cedars, the Lord breaks the ends. Pieces The Cedars of Lebanon.*

God is so big; He is so amazing. His Voice is upon the waters; the Voice of the Almighty Thunders. The Voice of God could scare the beejeebies out of you just by being God. That God would patiently sit with me or you and wait with us while we wait on Him and speak to us gently and with loving kindness is miraculous.

People think that when you pray you must yell, scream and holler. Well, yes if you are doing deliverance and you are trying to scare demons out of their close places. But I commune with God at night on my bed—do you think I'm lying in bed yelling?

Oh please.

There is a time and a place for everything. There is spiritual decorum, and there are fleshly theatrics. Know when, know which and seek the face and the heart of God.

So, you've prayed inside in your outside voice. When God answers you, is He yelling at you? God has only yelled at me twice, and I needed yelling at, but for the most part God speaks very gently to me, like a Good Shepherd leading and guiding, nudging, directing, gathering.

He is Wonderful. Thank You, Lord.

We need to learn how to hear our own spirit man. And as we spend more and more time in the presence of God and with the Holy Spirit our spiritual growth becomes more evident. And then when we're growing spiritually. Know the voice of your own spirit versus the voice of some other *spirit, or* the voice of some other aspect of yourself.

We must let Peace be our umpire in that. When we have Peace over a matter, then we know that it was God, it was the Holy Spirit, it was Jesus. It was the Prince of Peace. Yes, you may already know how to hear the *voice* of your own soul. Be discerning; there are people who are overrun by their emotions. And there are people who answer to their emotions all day, every day, all night, every night. Whether they're awake or not.

Remember in our dreams we act and we make decisions in our dreams and those are real actions.

I think of the TV show, Judge Judy. People come into a court and they decide they're going to defend themselves. They usually open with this line that they probably practiced and rehearsed. They'll start out saying something like, I *feel* that I don't owe that $5000 to my ex.

Judge Judy rolls her eyes and immediately interrupts and says, *Well, your feelings don't have anything to do with this.*

And that's real talk. You see if our feelings are hurt because we owe money to people, Let's say it's $500, not 5000. Let's say we owe $500 to the electric company; therefore, our feelings are hurt. Feelings don't change anything; we still owe it. Our feelings are hurt because owing money, owing people, and even spending money is emotionally painful. It affects our emotions.

Having to give away something you don't want to give away is emotionally painful. Having to share something you don't want to share, also emotionally painful. Having to sometimes do things you don't want to do. It's emotionally painful--, especially spending money paying for things. Spending money is emotionally painful for a whole lot of people. But it doesn't get us off the hook. We still have to pay bills, and that's more real talk.

The will of a man may say, *I want to do what I want when I want.* This is the mantra of a rebellious, stubborn, spoiled youngster. The mantra of a tantrum thrower is usually, *It's my way or the highway.*

The Counsel of Two or Three

In the counsel of two or three, let every word, and every decision be established. And let Peace be your umpire. The third aspect of the soul is the intellect. Soul-wise, it is the third counsellor.

Where no counsel is, the people fall: but in the multitude of counsellors there is safety.
(Proverbs 11:14)

Kids, stay in school. Read your books. Stay on top of current events. Intellect is good, it is needed; it's good to be smart. But the things of God are foolishness to the unsaved carnal mind, even if he's smart, (1 Corinthians 21:4). The things of God are spiritually discerned. And it's not computed in your brain. No. Stay smart. Don't lean always to just your understanding, but in all your ways, acknowledge God and He will direct your paths, (Proverbs 25:2).

It is the glory of God to conceal a thing, but the honor of a kings is to search out a matter. The first part of research is to ask God and then listen. This could save you money and time. It could save your marriage, your family, your career. It could save you a whole lot of hurt. It could save even your life and the lives of others.

We all probably know how to hear the *voice* of our flesh. In our bodies we have what's called a *steady state*. I am describing it slightly differently than what it would be physiologically, but a steady state is how your body is, how you feel, **usually**. When your body is working as it should, or optimally, and it's working the way that you know it should operate we can call that a steady state.

If something is going haywire in your body, it's what you will be thinking about; you just can't help it. You'll be thinking about it all day. Thoughts or feelings such as: *Why is this not working? Why does this feel funny? What was that pain? What was that muscle spasm? What's going on with my toe?* Those feelings are changes in what and how your body usually feels.

Yes, there are things that we just take for granted with our body. For example, most people eat food every day, but they shouldn't have to think about each tooth as they are eating. But if a tooth is not working, if it's chipped or broken, or if it hurts, you will think about it; that tooth will demand **worship**. It'll be all you can think about. And if you have more than one thing hurting, all you can feel is the thing that hurts the most. That is a proven fact.

So, if anything in your body or about your body is out of whack you will pay close attention to it, and you should so you can solve the problem and get rid of the issue at its very root, prayerfully. Pain is designed to get your attention, to save your life, really. If you feel dizziness, soreness, stiffness in your body, muscle spasms, or anything like that. And if you're wise, you will search out the root cause of that matter and correct it.

But if you're just flesh-minded or now minded, you just might say, *"Oh, I'll just take this medicine, or prescription, to fix these symptoms."* You'll get your comfort and your immediate relief even though it's temporary.

Fixing symptoms only can be dangerous, but if you can solve the issue and put your body back right again, that's the wisest thing to do.

A Magnum of Flesh

When you minister to or give in to the flesh you may find yourself participating in any or many of the following activities and all of these activities can make flesh very happy.

Now the works of the flesh are evident, Adultery, fornication, uncleanness, lewdness, idolatry, sorcery, hatred, contentions, jealousies, outburst of wrath, selfish ambitions, dissensions, heresies, murders, drunkenness, revelries and the like of which I tell you beforehand, just as I told you in time past, that those who practice such things will not inherit the Kingdom of God, (Galatians 5:19-21).

The works of the flesh satisfy the flesh, temporarily. The flesh is temporal. The flesh is now. The flesh wants to be satisfied all the time, unless you bring it under control. The flesh will consume your day, and night. It says, *I'm hungry*, so you eat to please the flesh. I'm thirsty, so you drink to the flesh. I'm sleepy, so you turn over and keep sleeping.

Flesh is not leaving the planet so it's not the wisest part of yourself to invest or over-invest in. Don't let the flesh keep you in bed when you should get up. Stay in school. Because the flesh is all about the party. The flesh is about the comfort, the flesh is about the fun, and the flesh is about the now. Consequences are usually not considered. Flesh is very now minded. It doesn't really know anything, but it thinks it does.

Several years ago, I saw with my very own eyes a young lady drinking an entire magnum of wine. I had to think back on the fact that she had drank that much wine, because she wasn't obvious--, she was sneaky about it.

A bottle of wine is 25 oz. No one person should drink a whole bottle of wine. We drink communion, that's about it for those who drink real wine. Most people use alcohol-free wine. You could get substitutes such as grape juice. Where a bottle of wine is 25 oz. A magnum of wine is 50 oz. It's the equivalent of two whole bottles of wine. And I want to add here a gallon of liquid is 64 ounces.

Now back to the story. Some years ago, I saw with my own eyes I saw a young lady finish off an entire Magnum of wine. Then after she drank the wine, she drank some margaritas. I think I saw her drink a couple of those. It was at a holiday office party, and it wasn't even her workplace--, she was somebody's guest.

It just dawned on me that I don't even know what she drank *before* the wine. Anyhow, the next morning she didn't understand why she had a headache, and she really, desperately just needed something for her headache. She was so perplexed, because what is this headache about? Where had it come from, she queried anyone in her presence. She really believed that she was the victim of some random headache.

She surely remembered that she drank and drank, because I found out that is her pattern. But she had no sense of the consequences of actions. That's the flesh. The flesh wants what it wants. It wants what it feels that it wants, and the flesh wants it now, and the flesh wants comfort, fun, The flesh wants to party. And then if you have bad consequences, then the flesh wants someone to fix it.

Even though Deuteronomy says you must choose who you gonna serve, consequences are outlined in the Bible; if you do this, *that* will happen. If you sin, here is the negative stuff that will happen to you. You can't blame anybody. You have free will. **You pick.** *And what you pick also picks for you afterward.*

But when pain or disaster strikes, the flesh wants someone else to fix it. It wants a doctor or some pharmaceuticals. They think that's what doctors and pharmaceuticals are for. It's for their comfort and their convenience so they can still keep doing what they want to do. If a person gets in some type of medical trouble, usually a wise person will stop their behavior, so the condition doesn't get worse. Not the flesh. Not the flesh.

The Word of God says to control your flesh. Bring it under subjection. Under subjection of what? Under subjection of your spirit? Every time you act on your flesh and your flesh impulses, every time you do what your flesh says to do, you're building up your flesh. And then what do you have? A built up hulky bulky flesh, like a muscle builder. A muscle-bound bodybuilder.

With a flesh-bound life, then when you roll up on a spiritual problem--, and you will have spiritual problems, especially if you're a carnal flesh monger, you have not built up anything of a spiritual nature, so you don't have any spiritual know how or any spiritual weapons to fight a spiritual war. The flesh will not solve a spiritual problem in any lasting way. It can't be done.

If you're listening to the devil, knowingly or unknowingly. I mean, really, look at what we're born into. We're born into sin. We're born into iniquity. Unless and until we acknowledge God and we accept Jesus Christ as our Lord and Savior and invite Jesus in to be the Lord of our lives and start spending quality time with God, with the Lord and Word and the Word in praise and worship and resist the devil. We're just automatically defaulting to the *voice* of the devil.

Faith comes by hearing. Even if you hear devilish things, you could get faith for those wrong things. You may start to think it's gonna be fun, it's gonna be a party to do that, but it may not be.

We need to listen to the Word of God. We need to listen for the word of God. We read the Bible. We can listen to our pastors; we can listen to teachers. We can Listen to prophets, apostles. We can listen to people of the fivefold ministry. We can listen to even babes, because even out of the mouth of babes, God has ordained praise.

As we listen to these words, we have to ask several questions. Is this what God sounds like? Is this what the Word of God sounds like? Is there Scripture to support this? Has God ever said anything like this before? And if I act on what these words say, will I have Peace?

If there's Peace, then we know that God was in it. If what you picked also picks Peace and brings it to you, then we know God is in it.

Glory to God. When we're hearing from God, and the more we hear from God, the more we heed and do what God says do. The more we hear and listen to and for those words of God, the more we spend time in praise and worship, and the more time we spend in the Word of God and in prayer, the more we will hear from God.

And God will reveal Himself in new and exciting ways. We'll have that victorious, abundant life that Jesus came and died for us to have.

Imaginations

We are not through talking about imaginations that exalt themselves against the knowledge of God. First, we all need God-Knowledge. Fear of the Lord is the beginning of Knowledge, however, if we don't know what the Word of God says, we will not know when something is trying to exalt itself above what God has said.

The fear of the LORD is the beginning of knowledge: But fools despise wisdom and instruction. My son, hear the instruction of thy father, And forsake not the law of thy mother: For they shall be an ornament of grace unto thy head, And chains about thy neck.
(Proverbs 1:7-9)

We get the Word of God in us so we can know that what was said over us, even if it was said by the person that we love the most, an authority figure, uncle so and so, your parents, your best friend, or even our Sunday school teacher or pastor – *was that true*? Because if you heard it and believed it – even a blind witch can curse a person.

Apply the Word of God, rinse with Living Water, repeat.

Backstabbing, they smile in your face, the backstabbers. They speak what the devil imagines for your life. If you don't do anything about it, it is the same as agreeing with those dreams. You have to pray against all evil. If you don't cancel or pray over them, it is the same as agreeing with them. These are evil imaginations that must be cast down because they are exalting themselves above what God says about you.

Evil dreams are talking to you; they say you are defiled.

God says you are the righteousness of God in Christ Jesus.

God says you are blessed coming in and going out.

You must know what God says about you. Fear God, that is reverence, have respect for God and His Word, it is the beginning of Knowledge.

My people are destroyed for lack of knowledge: because thou hast rejected knowledge, I will also reject thee, that thou shalt be no priest to me: seeing thou hast forgotten the law of thy God, I will also forget thy children. (Hosea 4:6)

If you don't do anything about this, for your own sake, do it for the sake of your children. A lot of what is coming up against you came through your bloodline. *You* don't want to be the cause of the types of problems that you have coming at your children or your grandchildren, *do you?*

Any evil imagination that has solidified into a curse, a hindrance, a problem, or an obstacle that is holding you back or is destroying your life right now needs to be cast down. Have evil folks ignorantly, and unknowingly made a devil deal where their descendants can't get married? Stay married? Have kids? Have good kids? Have good health? Live long? Own a business? Acquire wealth, have wealth, enjoy wealth? Own land? Own a house? Get an education? If you are having struggles in any of these areas, you need to suspect evil foundation and/or evil dedication.

Saints of God, those are the imaginations that you take out your spiritual weapons for to cast them down and bring those imaginations under submission to the Word of God.

Take out your spiritual weapons while they are still imaginations. In everyday conversation people say we are to *dispel the notion* or *dispel the idea*. That implies two or more things. One, an idea or thought can be dismissed from a person's mind. Two, if something can or must be dispelled (dis-spelled) then perhaps a **spell** was involved in it arriving into a person's mind--, hence, witchcraft or devil craft was involved. If spells, hexes, vexes, incantations, et cetera were used, *evil imaginations*, what that evil human agent wanted to happen or be in the life of their intended victim were used.

To *dispel* something means to get rid of it, to remove it. Obviously, to *dispel*, means to dismantle or tear down a *spell*. Cast down a spell as soon as you know it is a spell, or even suspect it is a spell; this is why we stay prayed up. Words and thoughts, evil imaginations can create *spells*.

Three, the thought is from outside of the person, because who would cast a spell on themselves? While I'm sure it is possible, it is not the norm except in those who self-hypnotize, for example.

Jesus said that the words that He speaks are Spirit and they are Life. We are little *words* in the Earth so what we speak is also Spirit and it is Life. Spirit **creates**. If something is given life, that means that what is created is sustained, it lives.

It is so much easier to cast down an imagination before it becomes what the words have framed it to become. The reason you have problems emanating from your bloodline is that you ancestors didn't do that. They didn't either because they were evil, didn't know that an imagination had been cast against them, or didn't even know where to start. Thank God for Wisdom and Knowledge; we know so much more now.

Get out your spiritual weapons and fight! Cast down every evil imagination, now!

How Do You Know?

How do you know if people are devising evil plans against you?

You sense *monitoring spirits* around you? They are around you for a reason. They've been sent, or they are on their own evil mission.

You may feel troubled in your spirit, vexed is what my mother would call it, a vexation of spirit. That person is feeling the presence of or under the influence of some negative *spirit*. (Isaiah 41:10-12).

You know that guilty person that can't look you in the eye anymore. People do that when they are talking about you behind your back. But they do it all the more when they are scheming evil against you.

People are quick to think just because you're nice and kind does not make you easy or stupid. To be kind is a quality that we all should desire. I suspect that people who cannot be human and kind at the same time might not be of *humankind*.

Casting down imaginations means to disassemble, take down, demolish, destroy, break up, take apart.

Yes, your own thought life can be a hindrance to your successes in life, and we do take responsibility for our own mistakes, sins, poor choices, and decisions. Bad thoughts are empowered by forces of darkness.

Unfortunately, we can assist the enemy in building a stronghold—but if a stronghold already existed when you were born and has been in place for 500 years, you will need to do more than think positive. You will need to speak 10X what God says, but you need to **deprogram** the curses, and **dismantle** the power behind them and you will need those spiritual weapons.

Evil Imagination?

Because that, when they knew God, they
glorified him not as God, neither were
thankful; but became vain in their
imaginations, and their foolish heart was
darkened. (Romans 1:21)

Evil imaginations are the beginning of idolatry.

We sin with our own imaginations.

The person who is casting evil at you is sinning… have we not the right to address sin if we are the Righteous? If we are the Righteousness of God in Christ Jesus, then yes.

Fantasies of violence, revenge, and other illicit temptations are all sin. These need to be cast down.

At church? Are we to think that people at church might be casting evil imaginations?

Possibly. Ask God. Everyone at church is not saved; some are there on assignment. Everyone at church is not on the same level; some may not even know that they are blind witches/warlocks. Everyone at church is not walking perfectly in the Spirit; some need deliverance from works of the flesh. Those on assignment and those who are "saved" but not yet fully converted come to church for easy pickings because who has their guard up at church?

I used to go to a church that I would say I have to put on the whole armor of God to even go in there.

Wherever you go, wherever you are, be and stay prayed up.

Aftershocks

Now, after the spells and curses have been sent to you to afflict or even kill you, you begin to feel some kind of way. This is where your own imagination begins to kick in.

Outside of evil thoughts about yourself being sent to you, some have internal negative opinions of themselves. As a child you were either celebrated or tolerated. You were told you look nice, handsome, or pretty, or people made fun of you. They may have said you were funny looking or ugly or whatever things people say to one another as kids. And some of that was internalized, whether you realized that it got embedded into you, or not. Faith comes by hearing, especially if you are hearing it over and over again, it's going to get in there.

So the opinions you have formed of yourself over the years are in there.

Some of those opinions may be generational, ancestral where your family has a certain opinion of itself. On top of that what does the community think of your family? All of those things color how you see your family, yourself and those things cause you to have an opinion about who you are, what you can have, what you are worth, what you can do and what you can't do or have.

If anything you think about yourself, your family, your value, your future, your abilities... etc is NOT what God says it is an imagination. It is an evil imagination. Whether it was already in you at birth and childhood or your formative years, or whether it was sent to you by evil human agents, it has to go!

Everything that is not what God says that is now in the DNA of your family came from an evil imagination and sponsors more evil imaginations.

They say, *If it weren't for bad luck, that person or that family would have no luck at all.* God says, **You are blessed coming in and going out**. If you don't speak and counter those evil words, those evil imaginations sent, spoken, or cast against you, what *they* say, even though *they* are not greater than God will stand because no one said anything different. This is why we speak, decree, declare and pray--, and stay prayed up.

They say, *Oh, he/she will never amount to anything*. God says, **Everything you set your hands to shall prosper.**

They say, No one is going to want to marry him or her. God says that He will put the solitary in families and the barren shall have children and be keepers of houses.

They say? **God says**. Know the difference, and to know the difference you must know what **God says**. You must know the Word.

What they say, if it is not the Word of God *are imaginations to cast down* because they exalt themselves above what God says.

If you don't believe what God says that means you believe someone or something above what God says. That thing that is speaking or has spoken that you believe over God is an idol.

Thou shalt have no other *gods* before me is the First Commandment. Whatever is speaking to you that you are listening to, and especially heeding is a *god* to you. Those are *gods*.

The *gods* are speaking, sending thoughts, ideas, impressions, influences to man day and night. Jesus said, ***My sheep know My Voice and the Voice of another they will not follow.***

The *gods* have spoken; your ancestors heard *those gods*, believed those *gods*. *Which gods?* The ones they heard, listened to and obeyed or followed, and then took on the nature of those *gods* because people around you began to speak just as the *gods* spoke. A man can have what he says, as well, faith comes by hearing. Those things **spoken** in your family have become traditions in your family. Those traditions indicate what *gods* you and your family are serving. Those traditions tell others what you believe.

You Have No Idols?

What are your traditions? What is the culture of your family? Unless your family and family life look exactly like the Godly traditions in the Bible, all "modern" traditions are associated with an idol or idols. You have idols. If it isn't just like God and looks just like God, then it is like another *god* or other *gods*. There are thousands of little g, *gods*.

My Beloved is the most beautiful among thousands and thousands. (Solomon 5:10)

If you think in the natural only you may think of your spouse or intended spouse when reading that passage in Song of Solomon. But to aver that your Beloved is the most beautiful, wonderful, the most glorious among thousands— among *thousands and thousands*--, even 10,000 little g *gods*.

There is no other like God. Period

Anything you can't let go of is an idol. Hoarders? Idols lead to hoarding; hoarding leads to idols. Folks call them *collections*, but they are idols. Cars. Clothes. Shoes. Handbags. Coins. Money. Food, and even People. These are the Earth treasures that we are not to lay up for ourselves, spoken of in Matthew 6:19. Because man is a worship machine, those stored up things can easily become idols.

Idols spew out words, they give influences, inclinations, and ideas. They each have a nature, and it is the nature of the devil. Anytime you take on any aspect of the nature of idols, you take on the nature of the devil. The enticement and the invitation is always to sin.

Most pastors and teachers have taught that you are the problem, and *your* thoughts are the problems as if those thoughts came from out of thin air, from your corrupt brain as if your brain was born that way. Well, it was born that way because we are all conceived in sin and shaped in iniquity.

Then the ownness is put on the individual to put thoughts out of their mind. How? Outside of deliverance, if the idols sponsoring the thoughts are **in your soul**, how will they stop talking and stop influencing you if you don't cast them out?

Casting down imaginations and every high thing, includes casting out idols and demons in your soul that cause you to behave in a way consistent with their nature rather than the nature of God.

But he that glorieth, let him glory in the Lord

God is the Most Beautiful amongst all the little g, and fake gods. God speaks Truth, He is full of Knowledge and Wisdom. The little g gods attempt to exalt themselves against the Knowledge of God, and they only cast imaginations by their nature and by use of evil human agents.

END

Dear Reader:

We are blessed people, the blessed people of God and the blessed *future* people of God; accept Him today as your Lord and Savior. And then you'll know where you will spend eternity.

Even before then you can live the abundant life that Jesus came and died for us to have.

The Holy Spirit will bring recall to the Word of God to you when you need it. Get the Word into you, study to show yourself approved. Then, when any evil imagination is cast against you, whether you hear it spoken in the natural, or start to feel or see the manifestations of evil having been spoken against you, you can cast it down with the Word of God. You can win out over evil every time.

I bless you, in the Name of Jesus,

AMEN.

Dr. Marlene Miles

Other books by this author

(anti-bewitchment books and prayerbooks are pictured with links)

AK: The Adventures of the Agape Kid

AMONG SOME THIEVES

Ancestral Powers

Barrenness, *Prayers Against*
https://a.co/d/feUltIs

Battlefield of Marriage, *The*

Beauty Curses, *Warfare Prayers Against*

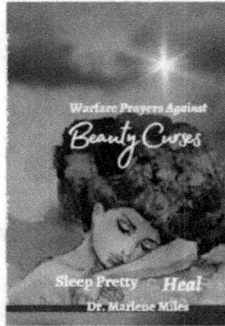

Blindsided: *Has the Old Man Bewitched You?*

https://a.co/d/5O2fLLR

Break Free from Collective Captivity

Churchzilla, The Wanna-Be, Supposed-to-be Bride of Christ

Courts of Marriage: Prayers for Marriage in the Courts of Heaven (prayerbook)

Courtroom Warfare @ Midnight (prayerbook)

Curses of Blind Men

Demonic Cobwebs (prayerbook)

Demonic Time Bombs

Demons Hate Questions

Devil Loves Trauma, *The*

Devil Weapons: Unforgiveness, Bitterness,…

The Devourers: Thieves of Darkness 2

Do Not Swear by the Moon

Don't Refuse Me, Lord (4 book series)

https://a.co/d/idP34LG

Dream Defilement

The Emptiers: *Thieves of Darkness, 1*
https://a.co/d/5I4n5mc

Every Evil Bird

Evil Touch

Failed Assignment

Fantasy Spirit Spouse

FAT Demons (The): *Breaking Demonic Curses*

The Fold (5 book series)

- The Fold (Book 1)
- Name Your Seed (Book 2)
- The Poor Attitudes of Money (3)
- Do Not Orphan Your Seed (4)
- For the Sake of the Gospel (5)
- My Sowing Journal

Fruit of the Womb: *Prayers Against Barrenness*

Gang Ups & Mobs: Touch Not God's Anointed

https://a.co/d/4bZoU12

Gates of Thanksgiving

got HEALING? Verses for Life

got LOVE? Verses for Life

got HOPE? Verses for Life

got money? https://a.co/d/g2av41N

How to Dental Assist

How to Dental Assit2: Be Productive, Not Wasteful

I Take It Back

Legacy

Let Me Have A Dollar's Worth
https://a.co/d/h8F8XgE

Level the Playing Field

Living for the NOW of God

Lose My Location https://a.co/d/crD6mV9

Man Safari, *The*

Marriage Ed. Rules of Engagement & Marriage

Made Perfect in Love

Money Hunters: Beware of Those

Money on the Altar https://a.co/d/4EqJ2Nr

Mulberry Tree

Motherboard (The) - *Soul Prosperity Series*

Name Your Seed

Occupy: *Until I Return*

Plantation Souls

Players Gonna Play https://a.co/d/1JrCNBT

Power Money: Nine Times the Tithe https://a.co/d/gRt41gy

The Power of Wealth *(forthcoming)*

Powers Above

The Robe, Part 1, The Lessons of Joseph

The Robe, Part II, The Lessons of Joseph

Seasons of Grief

Seasons of Waiting

Seasons of War

Second Marriage, Third--, Any Marriage

Sift You Like Wheat

Spirits of Death, Hell & the Grave, Pass Over Me and My House

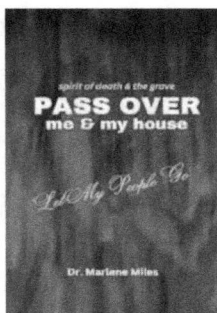

Soul Prosperity soul prosperity series 3

https://a.co/d/5p8YvCN

Souls Captivity soul prosperity series 2

The Spirit of Poverty

StarStruck

SUNBLOCK

The Swallowers: *Thieves of Darkness*, 3

Take It Back

This Is NOT That: How to Keep Demons from Coming at You

Throne of Grace: Courtroom Prayer

Time Is of the Essence

Too Many Wives: *Why You Have Lady Problems*

Tormenting Spirits   https://a.co/d/dAogEJf

Toxic Souls

Triangular Power *(series)*

- Powers Above
- SUNBLOCK
- Do Not Swear by the Moon
- STARSTRUCK

Uncontested Doom

Unguarded Hours, *The*

Unseen Life, *The* (forthcoming)

Upgrade: How to Get Out of Survival Mode

- Toxic Souls (Book 2 of series)
- Legacy (Book 3 of series)

Warfare Prayer Against Beauty Curses

Warfare Prayer Against Poverty
https://a.co/d/bZ61lYu

The Wasters: *Thieves of Darkness,* Bk 2
https://a.co/d/bUvI9Jo

What Have You to Declare? What Do You Have With You from Where You've Been?

When I Was A Child, *I Prayed As a Child*

When the Devourer is Rebuked

https://a.co/d/1HVv8oq

Without Form

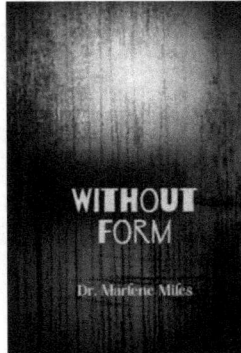

The Wilderness Romance *(series)* This series is about conducting a Godly relationship and marriage with someone who is a Wilderness person. It is about how to recognize it and navigate through it. These books are about how not to get caught up in such.

- *The Social Wilderness*
- *The Sexual Wilderness*
- *The Spiritual Wilderness*

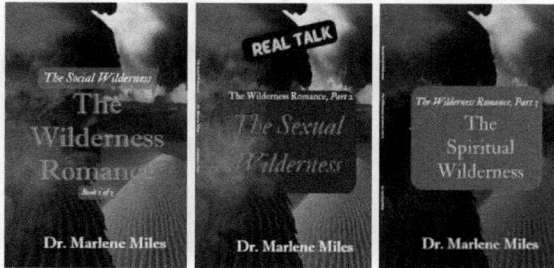

Other Series

The Fold (a series on Godly finances)
https://a.co/d/4hz3unj

Soul Prosperity Series https://a.co/d/bz2M42q

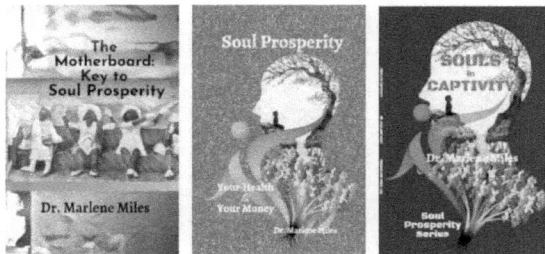

Spirit Spouse books

https://a.co/d/9VehDSo

https://a.co/d/97sKOwm

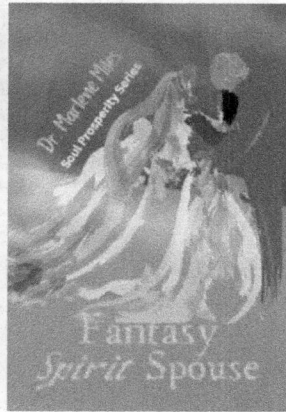

https://a.co/d/iTKK4f3

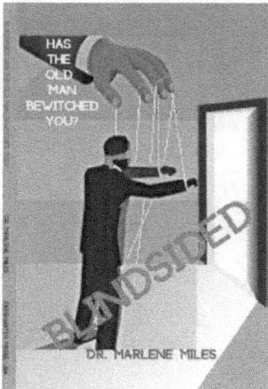

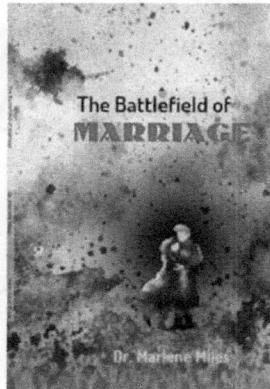

Thieves of Darkness series

Triangular Powers https://a.co/d/aUCjAWC

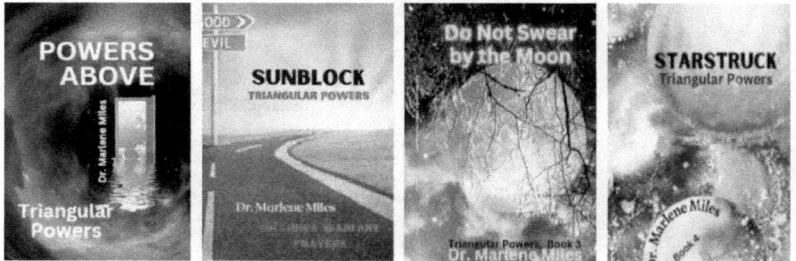

Upgrade (series) *How to Get Out of Survival Mode*

Notes: